Sounds of the Ferry

Written by Sara Leach

Illustrated by Steven Corvelo

Poppy Productions

Vancouver, BC

Poppy Productions
203-1328 Marinaside Crescent
Vancouver BC V6Z3B3
www.poppyproductions.ca

Library and Archives Canada Cataloguing in Publication

Leach, Sara, 1971-
Sounds of the ferry / Sara Leach ; Steven Corvelo, illustrator.

ISBN 978-0-9782818-2-3

1. Ferries--Juvenile literature. 2. Sounds--Juvenile
literature. 3. Ship sounds--Juvenile literature. I. Corvelo,
Steven, 1961- II. Title.

HE5751.L43 2011   j386'.2234   C2011-901066-6

Printed by Friesens in Canada
Manufactured by Friesens Corporation in Altona, MB, Canada
May 2011
Job# 64961

FSC
www.fsc.org

MIX
Paper from
responsible sources
FSC® C016245

Sounds of the Ferry

To Connor and Annie

-SL

To Cabral, my favorite picture book reading buddy

-SC

Engines **hum**,
Ramps go clunk,
Cars drive on, ca-chunk, ca-chunk.

Footsteps **thud**,
Steel doors *GLIDE*,
Children squeal and race to slide.

Churn Snap Hum Hiss Thud GLIDE ROAR

rEV GROAN zip Screech Clang Blow Snore

Steward speaks,
Big screws **GROAN**,
Whistle **BLOWS** its two-note drone.

Boilers *hiss*,
White wake **churns**,
Captain calls, the ferry turns.

Churn Snap Hum Hiss Thud GLIDE ROAR

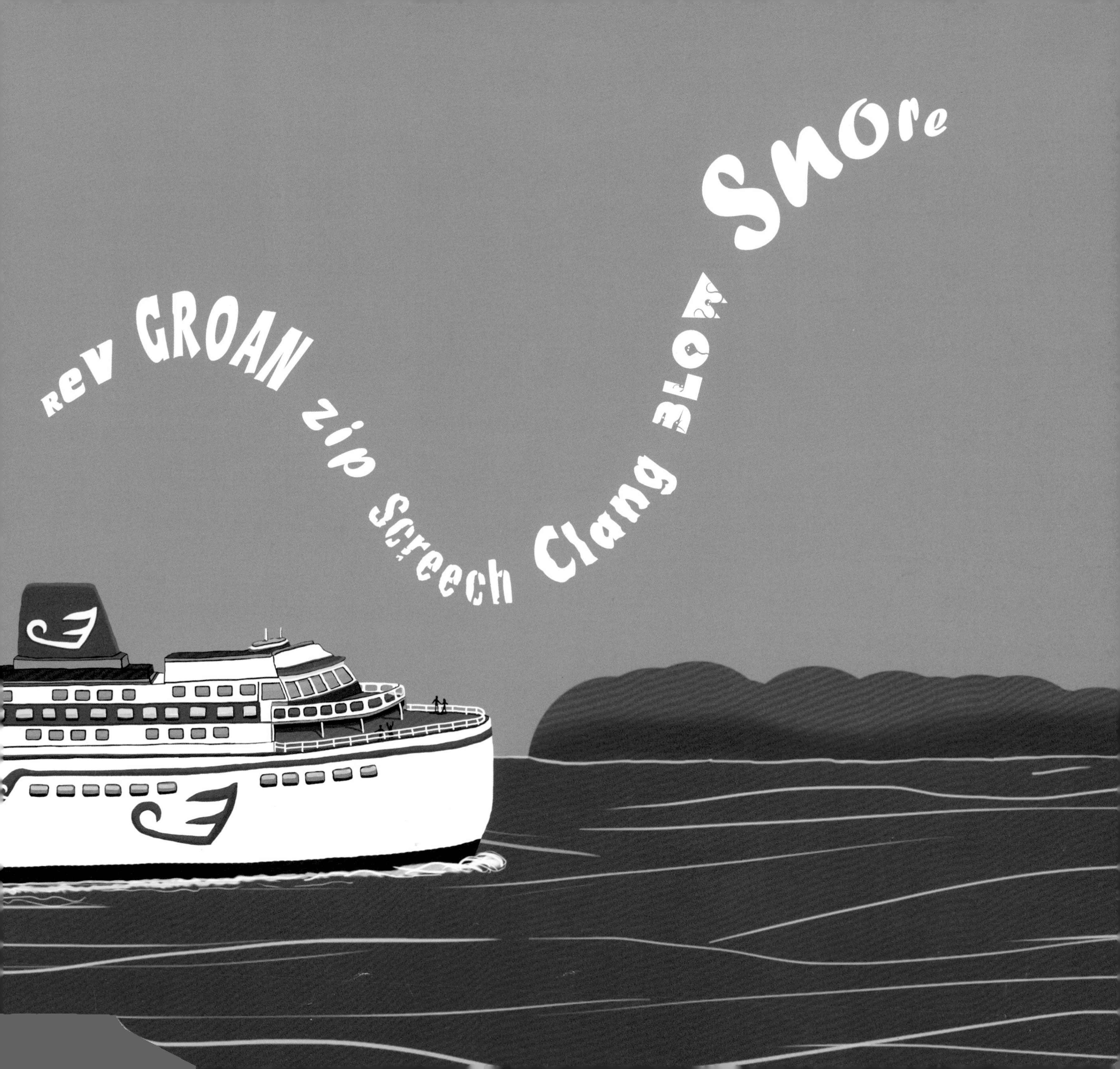
rev GROAN zip Screech Clang BLOW SNOre

Proud flags **snap**,
Seagulls **screech**,
Dolphins splash and orcas breach.

Grandpa **snores**,
Red card slaps,
Dishes **clang** by water taps.

Churn Snap Hum Hiss Thud GLIDE ROAR

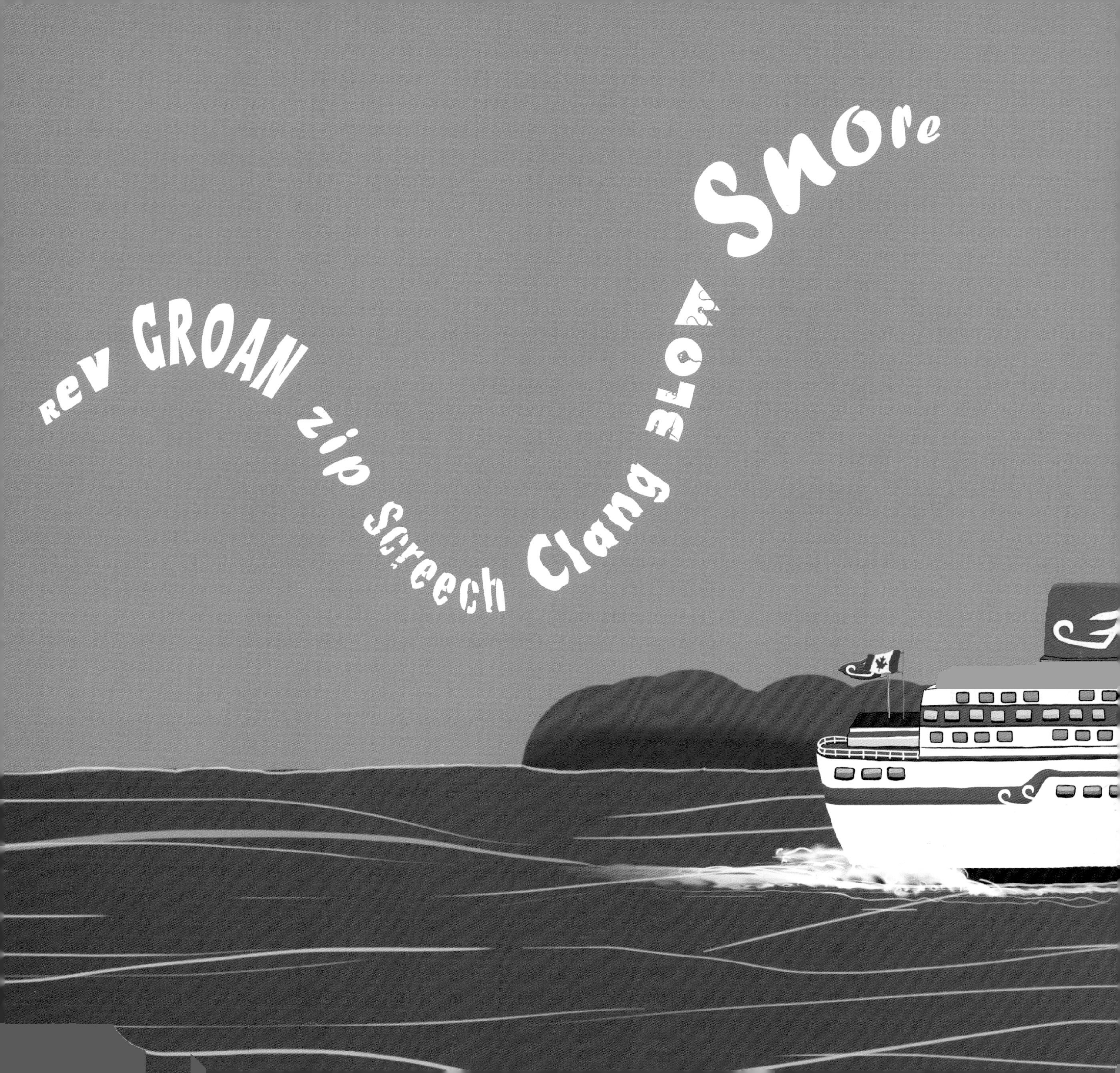
rev GROAN zip Screech Clang BLOW SNOre

Three bells chime,
Backpacks *zip*,
People chat and end the trip.

Tall trucks **rev**,
Bikes **ROAR** past,
Steward sighs, it's calm at last.

But . . .

Deck hands shout,
Cleaners sweep,
Busy ferries never sleep.

Can you find these characters in the story?

Sara Leach is a writer and teacher-librarian in Whistler, BC. Her books include *Mountain Machines*, *Jake Reynolds: Chicken or Eagle?* and *Count Me In*. She has traveled the British Columbia coast by ferry since she was a little girl.

Steven Corvelo lives in southern California with his family. *Sounds of the Ferry* is his second book as an illustrator. More of his art work can be seen at childrensillustrators.com.

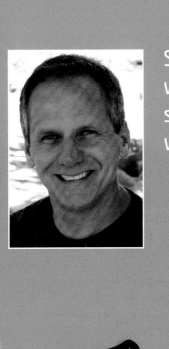

Special thanks to BC Ferries, Master Jan Bork, Senior Chief Steward Rod McNair, and the crew of the *Queen of Oak Bay* for the informational tour of your ship. Any errors are all mine.

-SL